CYBERSECURITY

CYBERSECURITY

Protecting Your Personal Information

Matt Doeden

LERNER PUBLICATIONS ◆ MINNEAPOLIS

Lerner Publications Company
An imprint of Lerner Publishing Group, Inc.
241 First Avenue North
Minneapolis, MN 55401 USA

For reading levels and more information, look up this title at www.lernerbooks.com.

Main body text set in ITC Garamond Std Book.
Typeface provided by Adobe Systems.

Editor: Anne E. Hill Designer: Athena Currier

Library of Congress Cataloging-in-Publication Data

Names: Doeden, Matt, author.
Title: Cybersecurity : protecting your personal information / Matt Doeden.
Description: Minneapolis : Lerner Publications, 2025. | Series: Gateway headlines | Includes bibliographical references and index. | Audience: Ages 9–14 | Audience: Grades 4–6 | Summary: “Cybersecurity issues routinely make the news, and their prevalence is only growing. Readers dig into the ins and outs of cybersecurity in this in-depth look at a timely and essential topic”— Provided by publisher.
Identifiers: LCCN 2024043539 (print) | LCCN 2024043540 (ebook) | ISBN 9798765669402 (library binding) | ISBN 9798765684153 (paperback) | ISBN 9798765677650 (epub)
Subjects: LCSH: Computer security—Juvenile literature. | Privacy, Right of—United States—Juvenile literature. | Data protection—Juvenile literature. | Data privacy—Juvenile literature.
Classification: LCC QA76.9.A25 D64 2025 (print) | LCC QA76.9.A25 (ebook) | DDC 005.8—dc23/eng/20250206

LC record available at https://lccn.loc.gov/2024043539
LC ebook record available at https://lccn.loc.gov/2024043540

Manufactured in the United States of America
1-1011882-53911-3/6/2025

Table of Contents

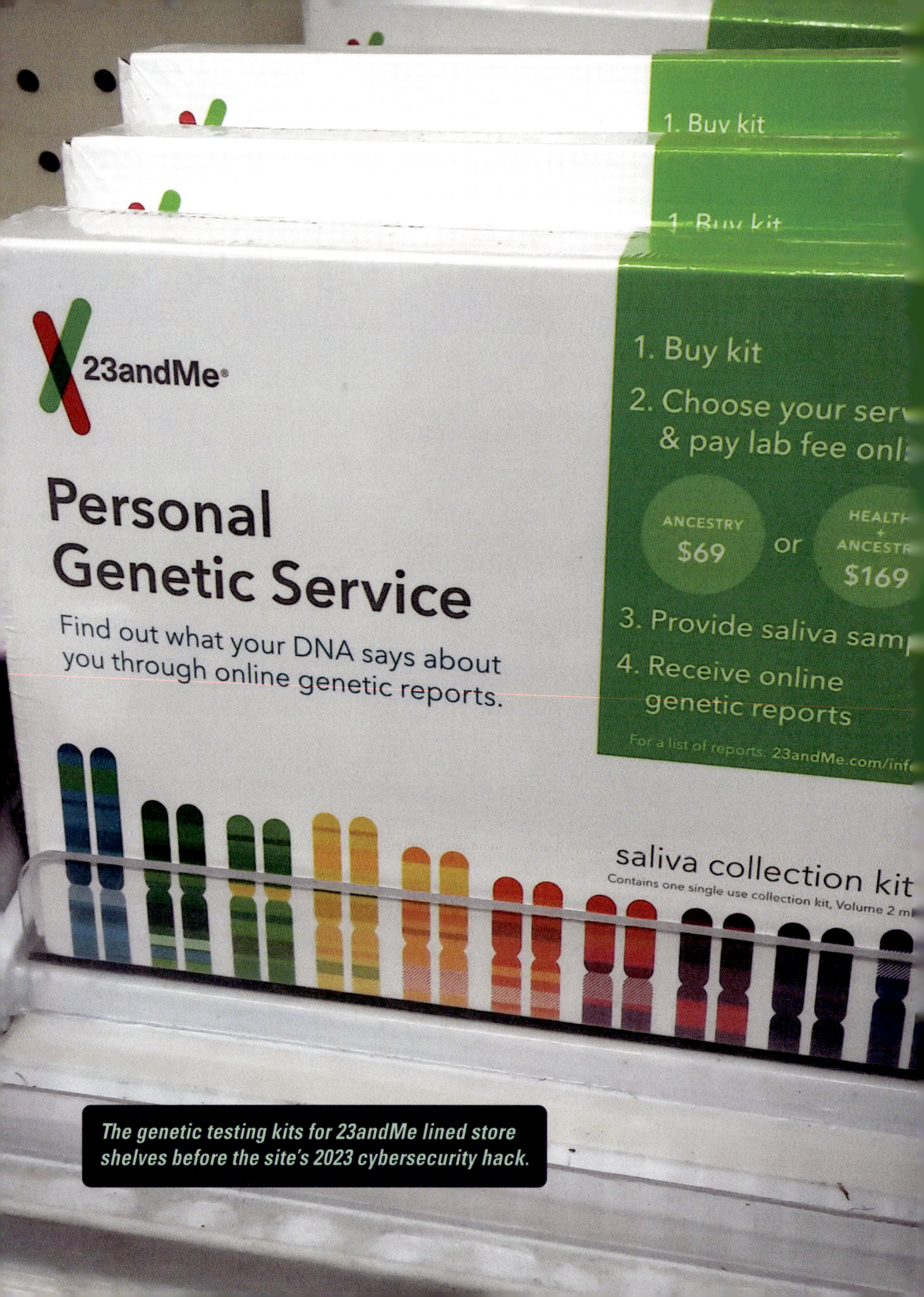

The genetic testing kits for 23andMe lined store shelves before the site's 2023 cybersecurity hack.

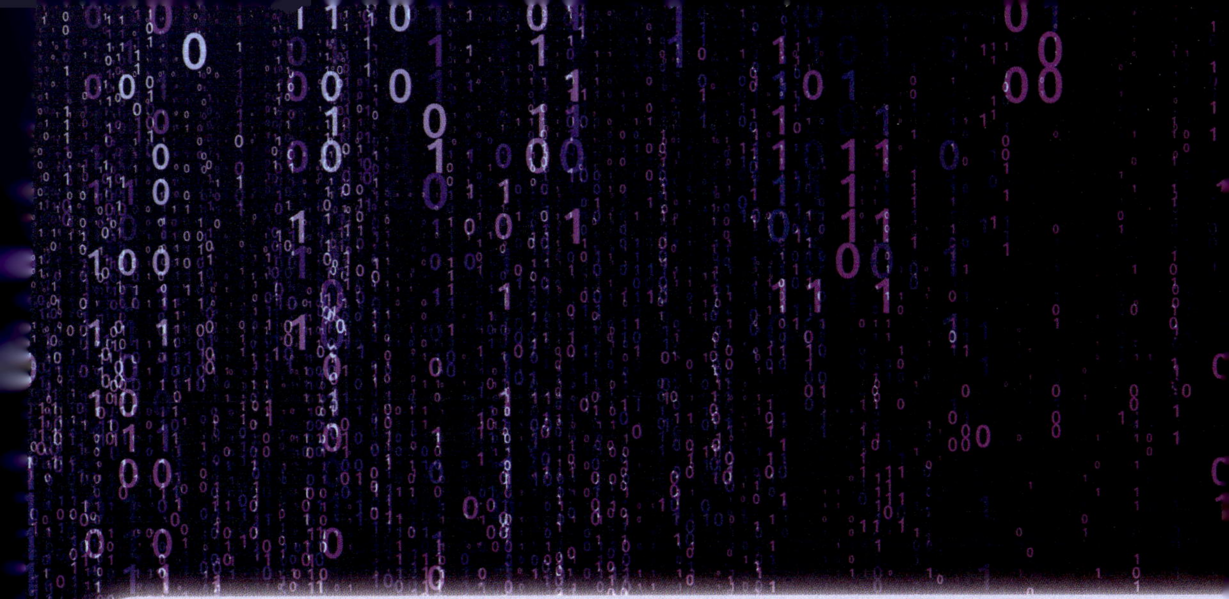

The news was shocking. In October 2023, the popular website 23andMe announced that hackers had stolen millions of users' data. The genetic testing site allows people to learn more about their ancestry and family history. Users provide a sample of their saliva. Then testers at the company use it to decode the users' genetics so they can learn about their ancestors, their ethnic background, and more.

The attackers gained access to a large amount of personal information. Users' genetic history, names, addresses, and other data had been exposed. Worse still, the hackers had put this sensitive data up for sale on the dark web—a secret corner of the web that's almost impossible to track.

For some, the possible sale of the data was alarming. In one post, hackers offered the genetic data and addresses of people of Jewish descent. That sort of targeted information may have opened doors to hate crime and harassment. "I didn't know [if] my family was going to potentially be a target," said one user of Jewish descent. "I may have put my family and myself in danger for something I did out of curiosity more than anything."

The company scrambled to respond to the attack. At first, they blamed the users. According to 23andMe, hackers blasted the site with known username and password combinations to get access. Because many people use the same log-in data for lots of sites, hackers who learn one set of log-in data can use it to break into other accounts. According to the company, it wasn't at fault for users who "negligently recycled and failed to update their passwords."

Others argued that the company was at fault. They said that 23andMe should have detected the sudden wave of unusual log-ins. It should have done more to protect users—even those who had failed to protect themselves by using unique passwords. They accused 23andMe of doing too little, too late and of putting their customers at risk.

The company did eventually notify all customers to change their passwords. They began requiring two-step verification (2SV). They invested funds in protecting their systems and data going forward. But that didn't change the fact that the hackers had access to many people's personal information.

While this was a big story in the news, experts in computer security were not surprised. Over the past few decades, the amount of private data online has increased.

Cybersecurity is one of the fastest-growing fields thanks to increasing technology across the globe.

Hackers target this data for profit. In a world that is more and more digital, people and companies must constantly work to stay ahead.

A booming field called cybersecurity is on the front lines. Experts in the field try to stay one step ahead of the attackers. But cybersecurity is about more than just fighting hackers and computer viruses. Anyone who spends time online can take steps to protect themselves. It starts with learning more about cyber threats, where they come from, and how to steer clear of these increasingly common attacks.

What Are Cyberattacks?

Legendary computer developer Vinton Cerf once said, "The good thing about the Internet is that everything is connected. The bad thing about the Internet is that everything is connected." Cerf believes the internet is filled with opportunity. But it's also filled with danger. It doesn't just connect you to websites and friends on social media. It connects everyone else with you too. And not all of these people have good intentions.

Computer pioneer Vinton Cerf speaks at Google in 2011.

The term *cyberattack* is common. But what exactly does it mean? A cyberattack is activity on a computer or network designed to collect, disrupt, or damage information stored on computers. Some even damage the computers themselves.

Hackers use a variety of ways, or vectors, to get into computers and networks. Sometimes they guess a person's password. They may use a username and password that has leaked online. Others use malware to attack computers. Malware is software that secretly runs harmful processes. Hackers can sneak it into software that looks real, or they may trick people into using it. Spyware is a type of malware that allows hackers to spy on a user. They can use it to steal information such as log-in credentials.

Ransomware is often considered the most dangerous type of malware. It can completely lock users out of their systems. The program then steals the data on the computer and sends it to the hacker. These criminals then demand money, called a ransom, to unlock the system and return the data. If users don't pay, they'll destroy the data or publish it online.

Ransomware is one of the many kinds of malware cybersecurity helps prevent.

BITCOIN AND CRYPTO

Hackers who use ransomware usually demand victims pay them in Bitcoin or other cryptocurrency (crypto). Unlike paper money, bitcoin is a digital currency. It only exists in a digital form and is designed to be hard to track. Many people use and invest in these currencies for legal purposes. But their anonymous (often untraceable) design also makes them appealing to criminals. Crypto payments don't go through banks, which keep a record of transactions. Once a crypto transfer is made, it's almost impossible to reverse.

One of the most famous cases of a ransomware attack happened in 2017. A program called WannaCry infected more than two hundred thousand computers. Hundreds of people paid to have their data returned before researchers finally found a way to kill the malware.

Although WannaCry infected personal computers, other attacks focus on bigger targets such as company websites and servers. Denial-of-service attacks flood a server with requests. The server can't handle the online traffic. It slows to a crawl or even stops completely. Users then can't use the site or server.

Networks carry data from computer to computer. Hackers often target them. They get access to steal or change information as it passes through the network.

Often the victim has no idea that the attacker is even there.

These are just a few of the most common types of cyberattacks. Hackers can use any weakness in a system to get inside. Both individuals and companies need to defend themselves and make sure hackers cannot access data.

The History of Cyberattacks

Computer networks have been around since the 1950s. But those early networks were slow and clunky. Most people didn't have access to computers, so there was little need for high-tech security.

Early computer networks were much less sophisticated than modern-day technology.

In the 1970s, things began to change. The modern internet did not exist yet. But computers had grown more widespread. More of them were connected to big networks. This got computer programmer Bob Thomas thinking about the dangers posed by computers being linked to one another. He wondered if a small computer program could spread from computer to computer on its own. In 1971 he built a program called Creeper to test the idea. It was a type of computer virus that modern-day experts call a worm.

Creeper worked. It jumped from computer to computer on a small network, just as Thomas had planned. But Creeper didn't stop there. The first version of Creeper just moved around. But a later version also made copies of itself. That meant it could spread easily and quickly.

Creeper may have been the world's first computer virus, but it didn't cause any harm. The program was built only to show that networks were at risk of attacks. And it gave birth to the first antivirus software. A new program called Reaper was designed to delete Creeper wherever it spread. The creation of a virus and of software to stop it was a glimpse into the future of computers. Creeper was an innocent test, but harmful cyberattacks soon followed.

One of the world's first hackers was Kevin Mitnick. From 1970 to 1995, Mitnick broke into some of the world's biggest servers. He tricked company employees into giving passwords that got him into secure servers.

Kevin Mitnick was one of the first computer hackers. He later became an author and cybersecurity expert.

The Federal Bureau of Investigation (FBI) arrested Mitnick in 1995. After serving prison time, Mitnick became a cybersecurity expert and author.

Early networks were not globally organized. Different networks communicated in different ways. There was no single standard. Most computers could not interface with others. In 1983 that began to change. A new standard for communication was created. Suddenly, computers all around the world could "talk" to one another. This global network is now known as the internet.

The creation of the internet led to widespread computer hacking.

At first, the internet was mainly used by researchers, educators, and students. But it became widespread in the 1990s. The internet gave people a world of information at their fingertips. It provided new ways to communicate with people all over the world without leaving home.

It also gave hackers a huge new area to explore. Computer viruses and malware lurked in the dark corners of the internet. Antivirus software grew

Computer users needed a defense from these harmful programs. In the 2000s, antivirus software became a must-have for anyone online. Reaper was technically the first antivirus program. The first real-world antivirus software appeared in 1987. Like Reaper, it was designed to get rid of just one virus, Vienna. Later that year, a new company called McAfee sold a program called VirusScan. It helped give birth to a new industry—cybersecurity.

McAfee is one the world's largest computer security and virus scan companies.

Other companies quickly followed with their own defensive software. Because threats were constantly changing, antivirus software quickly became outdated. If it couldn't stop the newest forms of attacks, it was useless. As using the internet became more common in the 1990s, companies started selling subscriptions for their services. They regularly updated the software to keep up with the latest threats. Customers paid monthly (or yearly) fees for cyber protection.

Network Security and Firewalls

Most malware directly targets computers, but networks are also at risk. This includes equipment such as modems and routers. These pieces of gear serve as a bridge between a computer and a network. Servers are also prone to attack because they store information and send it to network users.

There are two main types of network attacks: passive and active. Passive attacks are the most common. In a passive attack, a hacker gets into a network or server. The hacker may have passwords that have been leaked, or they take advantage of back doors into systems. These are ways to get past security. The 23andMe breech of 2023 was a passive attack. The hackers didn't change anything on the server. They just stole data.

Active attacks start in a similar way. Hackers break into a server. However, in an active attack, hackers don't just steal data—they make changes. They may delete data or create new data. Sometimes they encrypt data. Encryption is like a secret code. The data is still there, but it is locked away by a key. In ransomware attacks, hackers offer victims that key—for a price.

Because of these types of threats, a secure network is an essential part of cybersecurity. One of the most important tools for protecting a network is a firewall. Firewalls got their name from firewalls in construction, which are flame-resistant walls that help prevent the spread of fires. In cybersecurity, firewalls stand between a computer or network and outside connections. They monitor all the data going in and out, safeguarding the information. If the firewall spots something dangerous, it shuts down the connection.

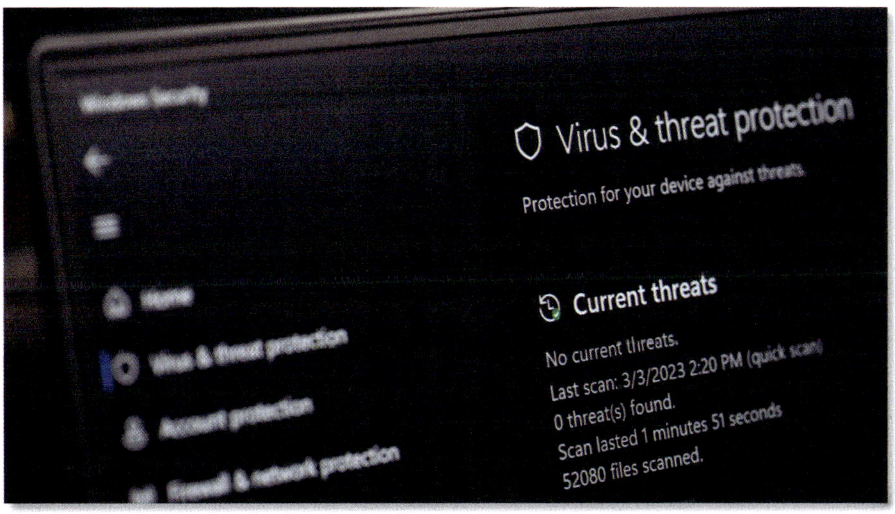

Virus protection software helps guard against potential threats to a computer.

A HACKER IN THE ROOM

In 2019 a couple in Mississippi installed a camera in the room of their young daughters. It was a way for them to keep an eye on the girls. But a few days later, strange things started happening. Music played through the speaker. Then a man started speaking to the girls. He even told them he was Santa Claus. The camera had been hacked. The family immediately unplugged it, but they learned a hard lesson: Almost anything online can be hacked.

The good thing about traditional firewalls is that they are inexpensive and easy to set up. They stop most of the harmful traffic, but they are not perfect. Hackers can find ways to get around them. While a traditional firewall might be secure enough for a home computer or network, many businesses need more.

Next-generation firewalls (NGFWs) are the next step. NGFWs are more expensive and harder to set up, but they are packed with extra security features. A traditional firewall scans much of the data coming in. An NGFW inspects every bit of it. Even skilled hackers have trouble breaking through them.

In recent years, even these more advanced NGFWs have been the victims of cyberattacks. Some security experts believe the age of the firewall is ending. They believe artificial intelligence (AI) is the key to future network security.

AI security works a bit differently. It relies on machine learning. AI figures out what a computer or network's normal use looks like. Then it actively monitors the system from within. AI can respond as soon as it spots something harmful or abnormal.

Security expert Nicole Eagan addresses an audience in 2019.

As security expert Nicole Eagan puts it, "The big challenge that the whole security industry and the chief security officers have right now is that they're always chasing yesterday's attack." That's what makes AI so valuable. Because it's screening for abnormalities, it can detect even never-before-seen abnormalities that may point to an attack. "This is just learning in real time what's going on," Eagan says, "and using AI to recommend actions to take, even if the attack's never been seen before."

Identity Theft

Think about the many businesses and websites that have personal information. Hospitals, schools, and government agencies are just the start. Have you signed up for online games? Do you have accounts with online stores? What about music services, streaming services, and social media accounts?

There is a lot of personal information online. And there are people who want to access it. People's Social Security numbers, phone numbers, email addresses, and more are on servers that are supposed to be safe. But history has taught everyone a lesson: Many of these servers are not as secure as they should be.

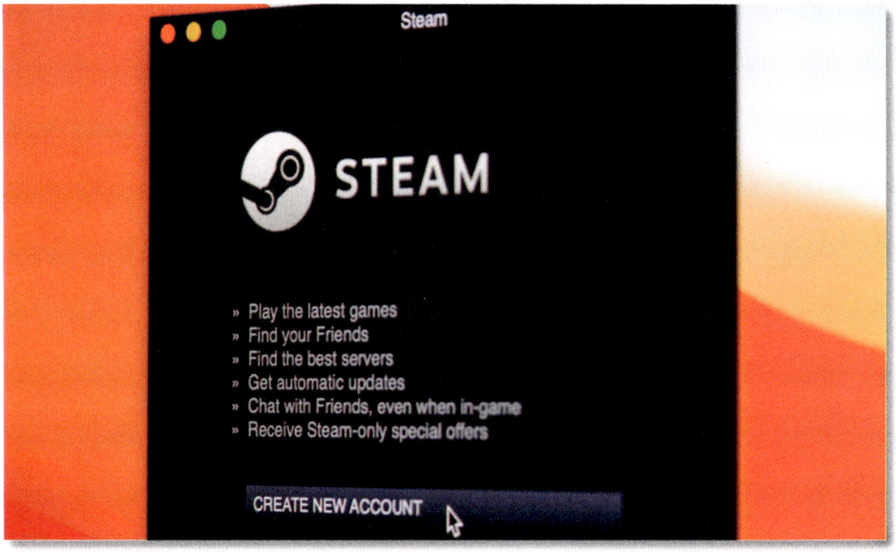

Hackers may break into online gaming accounts to steal users' personal information.

Why would anyone want this information? The answer is simple: identity theft. Identity theft allows criminals to use the information people give when they sign up for things—from credit cards to streaming services. They may want to spam you with scam emails, texts, or phone calls.

In 2024 a woman in Omaha, Nebraska, was surprised to find a package on her doorstep. It was a brand-new Apple iPad. She had never ordered the tablet, so finding it on her doorstep was a surprise. She took the package inside. About thirty minutes later, a stranger appeared at her door.

Hackers have been known to ship items to an unsuspecting victim before collecting them from doorsteps.

The man was part of a scam. Someone had stolen the woman's identity and ordered the iPad using her name and account. They had sent the iPad to her home knowing that it would likely be left by the front door. Then they had hired the man who was standing outside to swipe it. His plan was to scoop it up off the doorstep before she found it herself.

Sometimes the stakes are even higher than the price of an iPad. In 2024 a Kentucky family was planning a pricey vacation through Carnival Cruise Line. They were so excited that they posted their trip details (including

A Carnival Cruise Line ship at port

their booking number) on social media. That was a big mistake. Someone used that post to steal their identity and log into their account with the cruise line. The thief canceled the trip. Carnival Cruise Line refunded the money—to the thief. The family showed up for their trip, but there was no room for them. Their trip was gone, and their money was too.

Some people lose even more in identity theft. Identity thieves can get access to bank accounts. They can clean accounts of tens of thousands of dollars—or more. They may take out loans in the victim's name or get fraudulent credit cards. Identity theft can cause chaos in victims' lives. People can often spend months or years cleaning up after the financial mess a thief can make.

Scams and Phishing

Everyone has heard stories of scams and phishing. Phishing is an attempt to trick people into giving a scammer their money. These scams work all too often. Phishing usually involves sending fake emails or other communications.

Scams are all over the internet, from fake products to miracle cures. Scammers may pose as a person desperate for financial help cut off from their funds in a foreign country. They agree to then pay thousands to anyone willing to give them a small amount of money in the moment. They just need that person's bank account information.

Phishing is one of the most common types of scams. The goal is to trick the receiver into believing that the email is real. One of the most common phishing scams is an email that looks like it came from a business, such as an online retailer or a bank. The message will often urge the reader to log into their account. They may warn of danger to the account or promise amazing deals.

These types of emails often look real. They use logos and buttons that appear similar to the actual site, but clicking on them may take you to a spoofed (faked) site. There, you will enter your username and password.

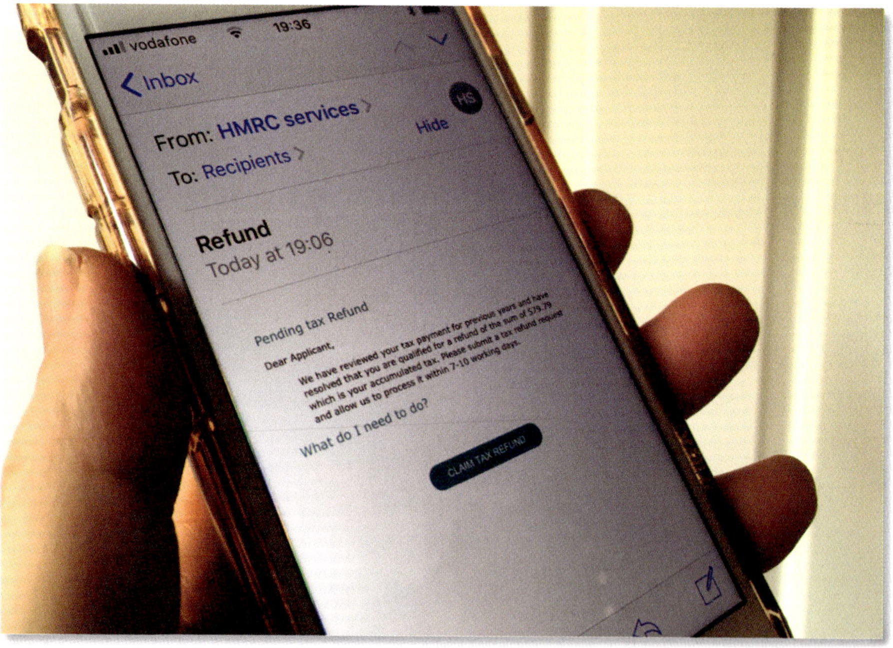

Phishing emails may look authentic, but they are designed to trick people into falling for scams.

Suddenly, the scammers have access to an account, including payment details and even banking information.

Charlotte Cowles was the victim of phishing in 2023. One morning someone claiming to be from the online retailer Amazon contacted her to explain that there was suspicious activity on her account. It looked like someone had stolen her identity to open fake accounts. She was led to believe she needed to speak to a federal agent immediately to undo the damage.

One thing was true. Cowles's identity had been stolen—by the people claiming to be helping her. Cowles was alarmed and a little suspicious, but she followed directions and spoke to the federal agent. He had all of her information—name, address, Social Security number, and more. He told Cowles that her identity had been used to commit crimes in several states. There were warrants out for her arrest. Criminals were looking for her. She was in serious trouble. Her life could be in danger. She had to act fast to clear her name and protect her savings.

Scammers could clear out her bank accounts at any moment, he warned. She couldn't trust anyone—not even her husband or the bank. Her calls were probably being monitored, so she shouldn't call anyone for help.

The fake agent told her to cash out almost everything she had and put it in a box. He would send someone to her house to pick it up and keep it safe. Crowles handed $50,000 to a stranger, believing he was helping her. And just like that, her savings were gone. She had fallen for an elaborate phishing scheme.

Installing antivirus software is one important way to prevent hacking.

In 2021 Marjorie Bloom also lost her savings to a phishing scam. A pop-up ad on her computer looked like a security threat. Bloom followed up with a "tech support" team. She ended up talking to someone who claimed to be a fraud investigator from her bank. The scammer told her to put all of her savings—more than $600,000—into cryptocurrency. It would be safer there, he assured her. When she did, he stole all of it. Bloom had worked her entire life to save for retirement. Suddenly, it was all gone.

Being Cyber Smart

Sometimes it feels like cyber threats are around every corner. Scammers are constantly looking for victims, so what can people do to be safe? They need to think about how they use the internet and what information to reveal. One of the most basic steps to take in online safety is having at least basic protection on devices like phones, laptops, and tablets.

Antivirus software detects most malware. It will warn the user if it spots any. It usually has the tools needed to disable it. A personal firewall can also help. Firewalls are not perfect, but they do protect from many online threats. Finally, keep all software updated. Most software companies release updates, or patches, that fix known problems.

Smart password use is just as important. Having lots of usernames and passwords can be difficult. Nobody can remember dozens—or even hundreds—of unique passwords. Every site requires something a bit different—certain lengths, use of uppercase letters,

Passwords should be unique and changed frequently.

or special characters, and more. Sometimes people get frustrated and choose passwords that are too simple or obvious. Using basic passwords such as *password*, *1234*, or your name or date of birth is never a good idea. They are just too easy for hackers to guess.

Many people choose a secure password, but they use it for many different sites. It is a lot easier to remember one good password than dozens. The trouble is if it leaks, hackers suddenly have access to many different accounts.

Many sites offer two-factor authentication (2FA), or multi-factor authentication (MFA), for logging in. This is an extra layer of security that is much harder to hack.

Two-factor authentication makes hacking harder.

You still need the usual username and password, but when you use them to log in, a new step in the log-in process pops up. Often, a user gets a text, a call, or an email. The message will include a passcode that you have to enter before you can log in. So, unless a hacker has access to your phone or email account, they can't hack you even with your password. It can feel like a pain sometimes to do almost two separate log-ins, but it's worth the extra step to keep information secure.

Everyone needs to find their own system for making and tracking secure passwords. Maybe it's a sheet of paper in a desk drawer or a secure text file on a computer. Or maybe it's special password-keeping software. Whatever you use, keep it hidden. And be sure to make a backup copy. Losing your passwords can be frustrating. Biometric log-ins such as fingerprints and facial or voice recognition are unique to every user. They are faster and safer than traditional password methods. If this security tool is available, it is the most secure.

Protecting yourself from scams and phishing is about being smart and even a bit suspicious. Be wary of text or email offers that seem too good to be true. Check emails for proper spelling, grammar, and punctuation. If you hover over or click on a link, make sure it takes you to a legitimate site, not a spoof. You can look at the site's address for clues. A site like "mybankname.com" is more likely real than one called "mybankname.com.hk." If in doubt, don't log in. You could be giving away your username and password.

WHAT IF I'M A VICTIM?

What do you do if you're a victim of a cyberattack or a scam? Act fast! Change your password if you still can. Contact the site or service that is at risk. Have it freeze the account. If your banking information or credit card numbers are at risk, call the bank or the credit card issuer. If you're a victim of ransomware, report it to the FBI or other authorities.

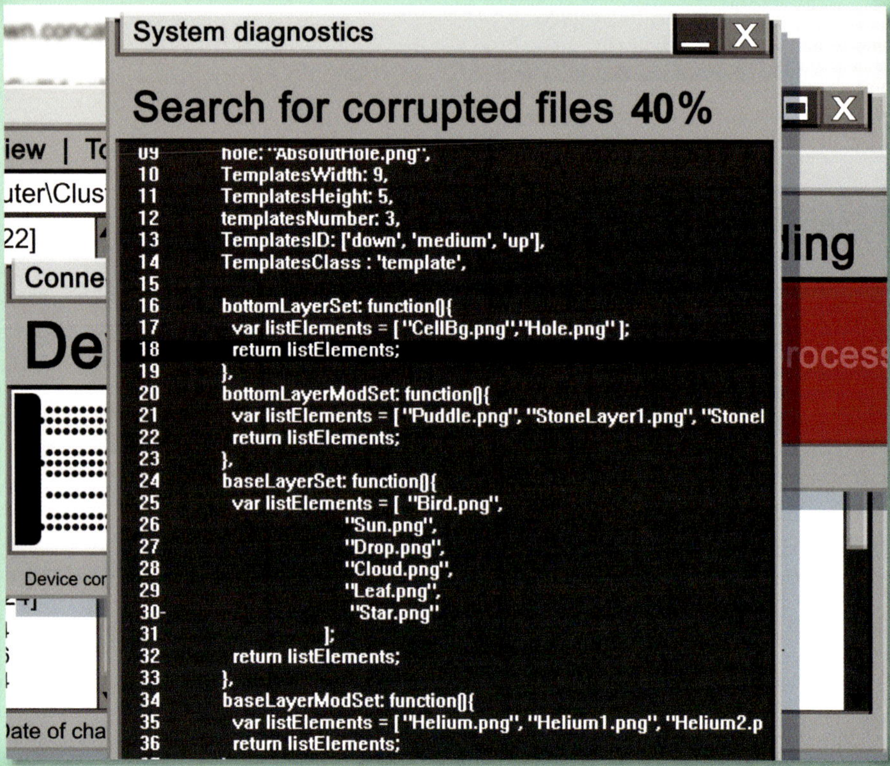

Corrupted files are just one result of a computer hack.

Make sure you know who you're connecting with before you give anyone access to your social media accounts.

Although social media can be a lot of fun, it's also a playground for scammers. They may try to friend you to get access to your friends list. Then it's easy to make a fake profile that looks like you and send friend requests to all of them. Stop them before they start.

Next, be careful what you post online. Never post details about your online accounts. Do not post pictures of airline tickets or hotel reservations, your address, or your school's location. Scammers can use this information to steal your identity.

Being online can seem dangerous and overwhelming. Everyone needs to protect themselves. Trying to clean up a hacking incident is harder than putting in the effort to be safe online.

A coder works on a security system to help prevent database hacking.

Careers in Cybersecurity

Cybersecurity is big business. Many companies have an entire division dedicated to it. According to Cybersecurity Guide, more than one million people worked in the field in 2023. If you enjoy working on computers or are good at setting up hardware and software, this could be an exciting career path in the future.

"We are fortunate now to have a ton of resources for getting started in the cybersecurity field," says cybersecurity software developer Josh Kamdjou. "There are lots of general cybersecurity courses, tutorials, guides, and materials available on e-learning platforms and online. . . . My advice is to seek these resources, as there are a lot of materials available out there that are designed to appeal more to people trying to test the waters and see if they are interested in the field."

So how does one go after a career in the field? Education is the key. The first step is to graduate from high school. Having a diploma opens up many more opportunities. Many colleges offer degrees in information technology (IT), with the ability to specialize in cybersecurity. If you follow this path, you'll learn more about how software and hardware are vulnerable to attack and how to prevent it.

Getting a degree is the first step to a career in cybersecurity.

There are lots of different roles in the cybersecurity workforce. Technicians do most of the hands-on work. They build and install security systems. They fix problems that come up.

A teacher speaks to his students about computer programming.

Engineers and architects design the systems. They plan all the parts of the security and how they work together. Some workers focus on investigating attacks. Others work with law enforcement to investigate crimes. Testers are ethical hackers. Hacking is their job. Testers try to break into systems to find their weaknesses. They report what they find to engineers and technicians so they can fix the problems.

Online threats are becoming a bigger problem as technology becomes more advanced. Criminals are eager to benefit from the personal information they can find online. And the threats are constantly changing. The rise of AI could help fight cyberattacks. It could also be used to carry them out. No one can be sure what the future holds, but one thing is certain: Cybersecurity has become essential in today's world. Technology progresses quickly and is an important part of our daily lives, both now and in the future.

Important Dates

1971 Bob Thomas creates the first computer virus, called Creeper.

1972 Reaper, the first cybersecurity program, is launched.

1982 Cloner, the first wild virus, begins copying itself onto floppy disks after being created by teenager Richard Skrenta.

1983 A new standard for computer-to-computer communication sets the stage for the modern internet.

1987 McAfee releases VirusScan, an antivirus program.

1995 The FBI arrests legendary hacker Kevin Mitnick.

The film *Hackers* is released.

2000 The ILOVEYOU (or “Love Bug”) virus infects over fifty million computers.

2004 A worm called MyDoom explodes worldwide, causing almost $40 billion in damages.

2007	Apple releases the first iPhone, giving users access to a computer in their pockets.
2013	Retail giant Target has a data breach that exposes forty million credit cards.
2014	A Trojan called Emotet infects personal computers and steals users' data.
2017	Ransomware called WannaCry infects more than two hundred thousand computers.
2022	ChatGPT showcases the potential of AI in cybersecurity.
2023	Hackers steal the data of millions of users on the genealogy website 23andMe.
2024	The FBI offers $2.5 million for information leading to the arrest of hacker Volodymyr Iuriyovych Kadariya.

Source Notes

8 Mack DeGeurin, "Hackers Got Nearly 7 Million People's Data from 23andMe. The Firm Blamed Users in 'Very Dumb' Move," *Guardian* (US edition), February 15, 2024, https://www.theguardian.com/technology/2024/feb/15/23andme-hack-data-genetic-data-selling-response.

8 DeGeurin.

10 "2002 Vinton Gray Cerf," Coalition for Networked Information, July 24, 2017, https://www.cni.org/about-cni/awards/pep-award/2002-vinton-gray-cerf.

18 Tim Matthews, "Creeper: The World's First Computer Virus," Exabeam, January 1, 2022, https://www.exabeam.com/blog/infosec-trends/creeper-the-worlds-first-computer-virus/.

25 Scott Rosenberg, "Firewalls Don't Stop Hackers. AI Might," *Wired*, September 27, 2017, https://www.wired.com/story/firewalls-dont-stop-hackers-ai-might/.

38–39 Sara Jelen, "Know Your Attacker: Speaking with Josh Kamdjou from Sublime Security," SecurityTrails, April 16, 2024, https://securitytrails.com/blog/josh-kamdjou.

Selected Bibliography

America's Cyber Defense Agency. Accessed March 11, 2025. https://www.cisa.gov/.

"Cybersecurity." NIST. Accessed March 11, 2025. https://www.nist.gov/cybersecurity.

Grimes, Roger A. *Hacking the Hacker: Learn from the Experts Who Take Down Hackers*. Hoboken, NJ: Wiley, 2017.

Ozkaya, Erdal. *Cybersecurity: The Beginner's Guide: A Comprehensive Guide to Getting Started in Cybersecurity*. Birmingham, UK: Packt, 2019.

Steinberg, Joseph. *Cybersecurity for Dummies*. Hoboken, NJ: Wiley, 2020.

Learn More

BBC: How Does the Internet Work?
https://www.bbc.co.uk/bitesize/articles/z3tbgk7

Britannica Kids: Computer Virus
https://kids.britannica.com/students/article/computer-virus/545139

KidsHealth: Online Safety
https://kidshealth.org/en/kids/online-id.html

Light, Charlie. *Outsmart Computer Viruses*. Buffalo: Enslow, 2024.

London, Martha. *Cybersecurity*. Minneapolis: Bearport, 2023.

Olson, Elsie. *AI Safety*. Minneapolis: Lerner Publications, 2025.

Index

Photo Acknowledgments

Image credits: © Richard B. Levine/Alamy, p. 6; Cravetiger/Getty Images, p. 9; AP Images/Tony Avelar for Japan Prize Foundation, p. 10; JMiks/Shutterstock, p. 11; European/FPG/Archive Photos/Getty Images, p. 13; AP Photo/Joe Cavaretta, p. 15; AP Photo/Hubert Link/picture-alliance, p. 16; AP Photo/Marcio Jose Sanchez, p. 19; Smith Collection/Gado/Getty Images, p. 21; Dzmitry Kliapitski/Alamy, pp. 23, 26; David Paul Morris/Bloomberg/Getty Images, p. 25; Angel Santana/Getty Images, p. 27; SeregaSibTravel/Getty Images, p. 28; Josie Elias/Alamy, p. 30; Mikael Karlsson/Alamy, p. 32; wera Rodsawang/Getty Images, p. 33; gahsoon/Getty Images, p. 34; Vladumir Kolosov/Alamy, p. 36; pixinoo/Shutterstock, p. 37; Roman Samborskyi/Alamy, p. 38; kali9/Getty Images, p. 39; LordHenriVoton/Getty Images, p. 40. Design elements: Golubovy/Shutterstock; SkillUp/Shutterstock; Kundra/Shutterstock; S and V Design/Shutterstock; In-Finity/Shutterstock.

Cover: Nwz/Shutterstock.